PING PONG

Rogelio Martinez

BROADWAY PLAY PUBLISHING INC
224 E 62nd St, NY, NY 10065
www.broadwayplaypub.com
info@broadwayplaypub.com

Cover art by Mark Bauhs

First printing: November 2016

I S B N: 978-0-88145-689-9

Book design: Marie Donovan
Page make-up: Adobe InDesign
Typeface: Palatino
Printed and bound in the U S A

PING PONG was first presented at the The Public
Theater (Oskar Eustis, Artistic Director) in February
2015. The cast and creative contributors were:

GLENN COWAN.. Erin Gann
ZHUANG ZEDONG ....Hansel Tan
NIXON.. Steve Mellor
KISSINGER.. Daniel Pearce
PREMIER ZHOU ENLAI.............................. James Yaegashi
CHAIRMAN MAO .... Ron Nakahara
JIA...Jennifer Ikeda
AUBREY... Clea Alsip

Director.. Kate Whoriskey
Dramaturg..Jesse Alick
Set designer.. Raul Abrego
Costume designer......................... Amanda Chandrashaker
Sound designer.. Nicholas Pope
Video designer...Bryan Maier
Movement director.....................................Warren Adams

CHARACTERS & SETTING

Glenn Cowan
Zhuang Zedong
Nixon
Kissinger
Premier Zhou Enlai
Chairman Mao
Jia
Aubrey
Nurse Wu
Reporters
Technician
Jim
Easter Bunny
Russian Waiter

The play takes place in 1971 and 1972. China and the United States.

This play is dedicated to John Clinton Eisner and The Lark Theater Company who gave me what every playwright craves: a home.

ACT ONE

Prologue

(Somewhere on the stage the following teletype:)

SUBJECT: CONTACT WITH THE CHINESE

REF: MY MEMCON WITH PRESIDENT SEPTEMBER 9

SUMMARY. I SAW CHINESE CHARGE LEI YANG AND HIS INTERPRETER THIS EVENING AFTER YUGOSLAV RECEPTION AND TOLD INTERPRETER THAT PRESIDENT NIXON WANTED TO HAVE SERIOUS CONCRETE TALKS WITH CHINESE. INTERPRETER SAID ONLY THAT HE WOULD REPORT THIS STATEMENT. I BELIEVE OUR CONVERSATION WAS NOT RPT NOT OBSERVED BY OTHER DIPLOMATS OR BY JOURNALISTS. HOWEVER, POSSIBILITY EXISTS THAT STORY MAY GET OUT.

GUIDANCE WHETHER WE SHOULD DISCREETLY STIMULATE PRESS INTEREST. END SUMMARY.

****

SUBJECT: CONTACT WITH THE CHINESE

REF: RESPONSE

WAIT. AND SEE

(End of Prologue)

Scene One

(1971. Nagoya, Japan. World Ping Pong Championships)

(Inside of the Chinese team bus. Everyone has their backs to us. Everyone that is but GLENN COWAN. *Dressed in tie dye leopard-like pants, long wild hair held at bay by a wide-brimmed floppy hat,* GLENN *is the quintessential American hippie. He has a small duffel bag. In his hand he has a ping pong paddle that he constantly plays with.)*

(For a moment GLENN *remains frozen. Then…he smiles.)*

GLENN: Outtasight! *(Beat)* Where the hell am I?

(No response. GLENN *looks around. The Chinese Nationals stare back.)*

(A TRANSLATOR *rises. The man is Chinese.)*

TRANSLATOR: You are in Chinese National Team bus.

GLENN: So you're all…so all these people are Chinese. And this is a bus. Let me just get this clear. Is this still Japan?

TRANSLATOR: This is Japan.

GLENN: For a sec I thought I was wiggin out. And you all play ping pong?

TRANSLATOR: Yes. We are National Team.

GLENN: Alright. Let me work this out. I'm American. I play ping pong. I'm surrounded by Chinese ping pong players. We're in Japan at the World Championships. And it's Saturday.

TRANSLATOR: It's Sunday.

GLENN: Okay. You see that's what was making things confusing. Now it all makes sense. I think now I know just—I am where I got to be. Now as that other guy says, You're either on the bus or off. So what do you say? I missed my bus and I need a ride back to the hotel.

TRANSLATOR: *(In Chinese)* He has no way back to camp because imperialists have no bus.

GLENN: That's right. Exactly what I said.

TRANSLATOR: You are fine to go.

GLENN: You want me to leave?

TRANSLATOR: To travel with our bus.

GLENN: Groovy.

TRANSLATOR: Groovy?

GLENN: It's going to be a gas.

(The doors close behind GLENN. *They're on their way. The people in the bus whisper.)*

GLENN: I know I look a little different…

(Whispers. During the following the TRANSLATOR *tries to keep up.)*

GLENN: A lot different? Okay. Okay. Yeah. I got it. No reason to flip out. My hair, my clothes. I'm still you. You're still me. We're on the same side. The people on top—they're the ones out of touch. My name is Glenn. Glenn.

(Silence)

*(*ZHUANG ZEDONG, *a ping pong player, approaches him.)*

ZHUANG: American Government unfriendly to Chinese, but every American is friend. I give you this gift to show Chinese friendship to American.

*(*GLENN *grabs* ZHUANG's *hand, shakes it, then puts his arms around* ZHUANG. ZHUANG *backs off but* GLENN *pulls back.)*

(He opens the silk weaving to reveal the Huangshan mountain range.)

(GLENN accepts the gift.)

GLENN: *(His face lights up)* Far out.

ZHUANG: Yes. Far.

GLENN: No. I mean. Far out. Like cool.

ZHUANG: Cool? Yes.

(Suddenly the bus disappears and the two men are surrounded by REPORTERS calling out for their attention. Flashbulbs. GLENN puts his arms around ZHUANG.)

REPORTER 1: Over here!

REPORTER 2: What's that you got in your hands?

GLENN: Mountains!

REPORTER 2: Show it!

REPORTER 1: Look over here.

REPORTER 2: Hey! A smile!!!

(GLENN shows the REPORTERS the silk weaving. Several more "Over here!" And "Turn this way" are heard. Then…)

REPORTER 1: You know who you're standing next to?

GLENN: Of course. Zhuang Zedong. This man here—world champ! No one can beat this man. I tried. I've been playing since I was fourteen and I haven't met anyone better. *(To ZHUANG)* I hope your team rocks it tomorrow!

ZHUANG: I wish you best. You impress me with your game.

GLENN: You watch me?

ZHUANG: I watch you.

REPORTER 2: Stand closer. Can you both hold—. Great.

(A new set of flashes. Suddenly, GLENN goes into his duffel and takes out a T-shirt.)

("Over here!" And "Turn this way" are heard before…)

GLENN: I just want to take this chance to give Mister Zhuang—is that good? Is that what I call you?

ZHUANG: Yes.

GLENN: I want to give him this gift. Everything I got to say is on that shirt.

(GLENN has a T-shirt in hand which he now opens for all the REPORTERS to see. It has a red, white, and blue peace emblem and the words LET IT BE emblazoned on it.)

(GLENN now turns to ZHUANG.)

GLENN: My heart, Mister Zhuang.

(ZHUANG accepts the gift and then…)

ZHUANG: Thank you for shirt.

GLENN: From Venice Beach where the girls are pretty and you can't go wrong.

ZHUANG: Venice beach where the girls…

GLENN: The girls are pretty. The girls are hot actually.

ZHUANG: Hot. Yes.

(Impulsively GLENN grabs ZHUANG and hugs him. The reporters snap away. Then…)

ZHUANG: These are very special mountains, Glenn. They are under water once. Now they touch clouds. Here one emperor entered heaven. The beauty is so great, Glenn, that one is forever changed after visit.

GLENN: Take me there!

(Suddenly, everyone freezes. The two players are caught in a camera flash.)

Scene Two

(The Oval Office. NIXON *writes in one of his favorite yellow pads. A* NIXON AIDE *is standing by.)*

NIXON: Dear Mister Presley. *(To* NIXON AIDE*)* Mister Presley or Elvis. How formal does thing need to be?

NIXON AIDE: Stay formal.

NIXON: *(Writing)* It was a pleasure to meet with you in the White House. I want to thank you again for giving me the commemorative World War II Colt 45. It is an impressive gift. *(To* NIXON AIDE*)* And I'm glad is out of your fucking crazy hands and in my sane hands. *(Writing)* Sincerely, President Richard Nixon.

NIXON AIDE: Very good.

NIXON: Stick it in an envelope with a picture of the family.

NIXON AIDE: With your daughters?

NIXON: What's that?

NIXON AIDE: You want your daughters in the picture or just you and Mrs Nixon.

NIXON: *(Beat)* Forget about the picture. Send him a pair of presidential cuff links instead.

NIXON AIDE: Very good, Mister President.

NIXON: He's been waiting long enough. Send him in.

NIXON AIDE: Yes. *(Goes)*

(After a moment, HENRY KISSINGER *enters in a stylish blue suit, he has a piece of paper in his hand.* NIXON *picks up the gun and...)*

NIXON: Bang bang! You're dead, Henry.

KISSINGER: Mister President.

NIXON: You don't ever smile, do you?

KISSINGER: I do.

NIXON: What do you have for me?

KISSINGER: I wanted to discuss an incident I've just been made aware of.

NIXON: Does this call for a double?

KISSINGER: Not just yet.

NIXON: All right. Let's hear it.

KISSINGER: A young Chinese ping pong player approached an American at a ping pong match in Nagoya.

NIXON: Ping pong?

KISSINGER: Yes, Mister President.

NIXON: Why do I care?

KISSINGER: The young man got on a bus—

NIXON: The American?

KISSINGER: He got on a bus with a group of Chinese nationals.

NIXON: And?

KISSINGER: Mister President, the Chinese don't do anything without thinking it through first. There's good reason to believe this encounter was planned.

NIXON: You think the Chinese are that clever?

KISSINGER: The Chinese can make the meticulously planned look spontaneous.

(By now NIXON has poured himself a second scotch.)

NIXON: You're right there. You never can predict the Chinese. The Russians I can figure out in a second. You can't do that with the Chinese. And that's only because they're Chinese, not because they're communists. The Russians you can read a mile away because they're doctrinaire. It's not the same with the Chinese. Subtlety. That's their thing.

KISSINGER: How do you suggest we proceed?

NIXON: Stay back but follow this thing. Don't make any noise whatsoever. And don't let Rogers and his cronies in the State Department pick up on this or they're liable to fuck it up.

KISSINGER: Fuck what up?

NIXON: I have no idea; but what I do know is that we nail a friendship with China and the Soviets will piss their pants.

KISSINGER: You're not being entirely realistic, Mister President. We have not had formal relations—

NIXON: In seventeen years. I know that, Henry. I was there for the break up. I was the Vice President or did you forget! I was making history. What were you doing?

KISSINGER: Harvard.

NIXON: Oh, get out of here!

(KISSINGER *makes for the exit.*)

NIXON: Wait. Stay!

KISSINGER: Mister President, I'm afraid—

NIXON: Courvoisier. Is that okay?

(*Beat*)

KISSINGER: Yes.

NIXON: An inauguration gift from the actor.

(NIXON *opens the bottle and gives* KISSINGER *a glass of cognac.*)

NIXON: A few years ago I was working in New York and a Canadian client was organizing a trade mission to China. He invited me to come, but the assholes in

Johnson's State Department refused to give me the
visa. I'm going to get there before this is over.

(NIXON *raises his glass. They drink.*)

NIXON: Who's the lady, Henry?

KISSINGER: What's that?

NIXON: Look at the way you're dressed.

KISSINGER: I am always dressed stylish, Mister
President.

NIXON: Don't pretend there's no one waiting.

KISSINGER: Jessica.

NIXON: And where is she right now?

KISSINGER: In the limo, Mister President.

NIXON: This is the old Jessica from a year ago? The one
I met at the White House picnic

KISSINGER: No. This is the new Jessica from last week.

NIXON: You love it, don't you. You bring them here in
a limo, they wait and wait and wait while you solve
the world's problems. They wait outside the White
House while you go attend business. This is all part of
the seduction, isn't it?

(KISSINGER *smiles. He knows it's true.*)

NIXON: What is it, Henry, the voice? Is it your voice?
It's your voice, isn't it?

KISSINGER: I don't believe it's just the voice.

NIXON: These two Jennifers you've known—

KISSINGER: Jessicas.

NIXON: What?

KISSINGER: The one you know and the one outside are
named Jessica.

NIXON: There was a Jennifer, wasn't there?

KISSINGER: There were three, Mister President. That I know of.

(NIXON *goes to reply but changes his mind and waves* KISSINGER *off.*)

NIXON: Get the fuck out.

(*Blackout*)

Scene Three

(ZHOU ENLAI, *Chinese Premier.*)

ZHOU: In the Han Dynasty there was a clever minister who proposed a set of ideas to tame those seeking to harm China. He called these ideas baits. He suggested that these enemies be invited and given the finest clothes and shown the great buildings in order to corrupt their eyes, the most delicious food in order to corrupt their mouths, give them music and women in order to corrupt their ears, and show them great favor by honoring them with an imperial reception party in which the emperor should personally serve them wine and food as to corrupt their minds. Afterwards these enemies will forever seek our friendship. Afterwards, they will do what we please.

(*Lights shift.*)

Scene Four

(MAO's *bedroom in his villa [House of White Clouds and Yellow Cranes]. To the side, a ping pong table.*)

(*A sleeping* MAO *suddenly startles awake. He has several I Vs attached. A heart monitor tracks his pulse.*)

(NURSE WU *rises from her chair.*)

MAO: The boy had leopard pants.

NURSE WU: Close your eyes. The doctors warned these new drugs you're taking have side effects.

MAO: No. It is the boy. Hand me the Premier's report again.

NURSE WU: *(Getting some pills)* Come. I will fix it. The little red pill will do the job.

MAO: What do Americans do at night when they can't sleep?

NURSE WU: Americans don't have these same advantages. The only drugs they use are the harmful ones.

MAO: *(Smiling)* You know just what to tell an old warrior, Nurse Wu.

NURSE WU: Open up, Chairman.

(MAO does. But then)

MAO: Wait!

NURSE WU: What is it, Chairman?

MAO: I need that report. Now.

NURSE WU: You must rest.

MAO: Do you want to join others in the wastebasket of our nation. *(Beat)* There is still plenty of room.

(NURSE WU hands MAO a piece of paper.)

MAO: The two with arms around one another. No past. Only future. *(After a few moments he puts down the report.)* Alert the Premier. Invite the American team.

NURSE WU: You said no to the Premier already, Chairman.

MAO: I am changing my mind.

(Lights shift.)

(A light on ZHOU)

ZHOU: Considering the American team's warm and friendly feelings, the decision has been made that we will invite them to our country.

(Lights shift)

(Oval Office. NIXON reads the note. KISSINGER stands by. This overlaps slightly with ZHOU.)

NIXON: ...we will invite them to our country. If they do not have sufficient funds, we can—. *(To KISSINGER)* They want to pay for it? What they think we can't afford it?

KISSINGER: Our embassy in Japan has contacted us twice. They want to know if visas should be given.

NIXON: What have they told them?

KISSINGER: We'll get back to you.

NIXON: How much time do we have?

KISSINGER: They want them there in a few days. The team's schedule allows it.

NIXON: A table tennis team is so busy they have to squeeze a trip to China into their schedule.

KISSINGER: I don't know.

NIXON: Did you just say I don't know.

KISSINGER: No I didn't.

NIXON: You did. I heard you.

KISSINGER: No. I did not.

NIXON: Yes you did!

KISSINGER: Mister President, have you read the report.

NIXON: It's twenty-five pages long. Half of it is the history of table tennis in China.

KISSINGER: There's one thing in the report that concerns me.

NIXON: Give them permission.

KISSINGER: You're sure?

NIXON: They make a move, we make a move, that's how it goes.

KISSINGER: It is my responsibility to tell you. The young man who began this. He's a hippie.

NIXON: A hippie?

KISSINGER: A hippie.

NIXON: You're kidding me.

KISSINGER: No. I am not.

NIXON: Find out what you can about him. Dig a little. Get your hands on his records. Talk to people who know him. Work a little, Henry.

KISSINGER: Mister President, this is a conversation you have with other men, not me.

NIXON: I'm not sending a nutcase to China.

KISSINGER: Not a nutcase. A hippie.

NIXON: They're one and the same.

KISSINGER: You should give this some thought.

NIXON: Send him home and let the others go.

KISSINGER: Mister President, he was the one who got the ball rolling.

NIXON: It's rolling. We don't need him.

KISSINGER: I believe not sending him would be a mistake. He is the heart of the team.

(Beat)

NIXON: Is he any good?

KISSINGER: What?

NIXON: Ping pong. Can he play?

KISSINGER: He's very good. For some reason the Chinese feel safe using a hippie as a go between.

(NIXON *puts his hand up. Enough. He thinks things over maybe even going so far as writing something down. Then…*)

(Beat)

KISSINGER: Mister President.

NIXON: What if this kid ends up doing something stupid.

KISSINGER: It will only be for two weeks.

NIXON: A hippie can ruin your life in two seconds.

KISSINGER: We'll make sure we have people mixed into the group.

NIXON: I don't want this decision traced back to us.

KISSINGER: What do you mean?

NIXON: Give them the visas but this never landed on my desk. You understand. Not a word. Let's see where it goes.

KISSINGER: Let it be.

NIXON: I don't need to hear that pinko's words in here.

KISSINGER: As far as the expenses—

NIXON: Pay for it. But the money—you understand it can't be traced back to us. Nothing.

KISSINGER: The Chinese will know.

NIXON: I want them to know.

KISSINGER: You don't want the decision or the money traced back to us but then you want the Chinese to know?

NIXON: We're still working the back channels. As far as we're concerned it's ping pong. Nothing more. That's the game they want to play, so that's the game we'll play.

(Lights shift.)

Scene Five

(Semi darkness)

(An airplane. A young woman, AUBREY, sits in the window seat. GLENN sits next to her. He is struggling with a camera, a Nikon F1.)

GLENN: Do you know how to use these things. I've been reading the instructions and I can't even figure out how to put the film in.

AUBREY: There are three reporters for every one of us and they still want us to carry these cameras around.

GLENN: It's fun.

AUBREY: I guess.

GLENN: Some guy with *Life* gave me some money to do it.

AUBREY: I know who you're talking about—Jim. Jimsomething. He did the same with me.

GLENN: Strange guy.

(By this time AUBREY has put the film in the camera.)

AUBREY: There you go. You can figure out the rest.

(Pause)

GLENN: That's it?

AUBREY: What?

GLENN: I thought we'd become friends. Explorers. Marco. Go ahead. You say Polo. Marco. Wow you don't give—

AUBREY: You're the question mark.

GLENN: What?

AUBREY: Before I met you they sent me a list of the team. There was Craig who worked—works for Ford. On the list there was a chemist, a university professor, a guy from I B M. Errol who works for the U N. And then there was you. A question mark. You haven't looked at the list? Next to your name. A question mark. Did you just forget to submit the papers?

GLENN: What was next to yours?

AUBREY: I work at a diner back home.

GLENN: It's a good job?

AUBREY: So what is it, Glenn? If you had done it. What would be there in place of a question mark.

GLENN: I go to school. Santa Monica.

AUBREY: You're still there?

(GLENN *sits down.*)

GLENN: Listen to this. I've been doing some reading. One of the guys on the other team gave me this little red book.

AUBREY: That's what it is The Little Red book.

GLENN: Yeah. A little red book. Look; it's full of quotes and important things. Now I'm not going to tell you I understand it all. "Anyone who sees only the bright side but not the difficulties cannot fight effectively for the accomplishment of The Party's tasks."

AUBREY: It makes sense to me.

GLENN: What party are they talking about? All over this book they keep referring to this party. What party and why haven't I been invited.

AUBREY: The Communist Party.

GLENN: Ah. Yeah. That makes sense. My whole idea of China is shaped by this little red book, so I've just been thinking it's a party.

AUBREY: You should start back at the beginning.

GLENN: That's what I'm planning on.

AUBREY: Are you worried at all?

GLENN: What about?

AUBREY: This trip.

GLENN: You don't go to a place like this and not come back different.

AUBREY: My parents are afraid I won't come back at all.

GLENN: You're still in touch with your parents?

AUBREY: You're not?

GLENN: Sometimes.

AUBREY: My dad said they'll let you in but they won't let you out. He's probably right.

GLENN: I'll make sure to get both of us out. If that's what we want.

AUBREY: You understand where we're going, right?

GLENN: China?

AUBREY: Communist China.

GLENN: We're just there to visit a few places, play some ping pong matches—by the way when you played that Swiss girl.

AUBREY: You were watching?

GLENN: You needed to go inside. With her long arms she had the outsides covered, but she was having a more difficult time inside.

AUBREY: Thank you.

GLENN: Just remember. With the Chinese it's a totally different game. It's the outside they have a problem with.

AUBREY: You're really excited about this.

GLENN: It's a second chance.

AUBREY: At what?

GLENN: I played Zhuang in Nagoya and I had no idea what I was doing. It's different now. I know what I'm walking into.

AUBREY: You have no idea, do you? It's not just some game.

GLENN: You're so uptight?

AUBREY: These people—they have no idea who we are and that means we have no idea who they are.

GLENN: What's wrong with that?

AUBREY: Two peoples that have not had any contact and all of a sudden—

GLENN: That's love, right?

AUBREY: I'm married.

GLENN: Of course you are.

AUBREY: Things don't change this quickly.

GLENN: Go with an open heart. You'll be fine.

(AUBREY *takes the book away from* GLENN, *annoyed.*)

AUBREY: The Seven Points for Attention are as follows:
(1) Speak politely.
(2) Return everything you borrow.
(3) Pay for anything you damage.
(4) Do not hit or swear at people.
(5) Do not damage crops.
(6) Do not take liberties with women.

(7) Do not ill-treat captives.
Does that sound like the place for you?

GLENN: I'll give it a chance. I mean there's no mention of drugs being a problem.

AUBREY: Maybe finally you can fill in that question mark.

GLENN: Listen to this one. "The world is yours, as well as ours, but in the last analysis, it is yours. You young people, full of vigor and vitality, are in the bloom of life, like the sun at eight or nine in the morning. Our hope is placed on you. The world belongs to you." That I understand.

(GLENN *tosses* AUBREY *the book.*)

VOICE: (*In Chinese*) It is with great joy Chairman Mao welcomes you to the People's Republic of China.

AUBREY: Welcome home.

(*The Romanian National Anthem*)

(*Blackout*)

Scene Six

(NIXON *in suit and tie is making a toast at a State dinner.*)

NIXON: President Ceausescu, Mrs Ceausescu, and all our very distinguished guests.
We are very honored this evening to receive the President of Romania. He is the first President or chief of state of a Socialist country to be received as an honored guest during this administration.
As we speak of the relations between Romania and the United States, we often refer to our differences, but on an occasion like this, I think that all of us are reminded of those things which draw us together rather than those that drive us apart.

It happens that in the world today because of the
divisions, there are times when the leader of one nation
does not have adequate communication with the leader
of another. But as I was saying to the President earlier
today, he is in a rather unique position. He heads
a government which is one of the few in the world
which has good relations with the United States, good
relations with the Soviet Union, and good relations
with the People's Republic of China.

And so for these reasons I know all of you in this
room will want to join me in raising our glasses to the
President of Romania.

(NIXON *toasts. We hear glasses clink.*)

(*Lights shift.*)

Scene Seven

(*On a monitor[s] we see the following:*
DAY ONE
Tshinghua University
Lecture on the Ways of Teaching and Learning
"Knowledge begins with practice, and theoretical knowledge,
which is acquired through practice, must then return to
practice." Chairman Mao Tse-tung)

(*Lights shift*)

(GLENN *lies back in bed reading* The Little Red Book. *Phone*
rings. And rings. And rings. And he picks up.)

(*A faint light comes up on a phone booth. The shadow of the*
White House in the distance.)

VOICE: Mister Cowan?

GLENN: Who wants to know?

VOICE: Mister Glenn Cowan?

GLENN: What is it?

VOICE: I want to let you know that Searchlight
views this mission in the People's Republic of China
propitiously.

(GLENN *has lowered the music.*)

GLENN: What did you say? What's that last word?
Proposetishious.

VOICE: Propitiously.

GLENN: Uh-huh. Okay. *(Beat)* What's that mean?

VOICE: Never mind.

GLENN: Who is this? Who's calling?

VOICE: Searchlight believes the trip—

GLENN: What's searchlight?

VOICE: Mister Cowan. Listen to me. We believe this to
be important for the greater friendship between the
two nations. If you were to get in the way—

GLENN: Henry Kissinger? *(Pause)* Is this Henry
Kissinger?

(Pause)

VOICE: No. It is not.

(Pause)

GLENN: Hey. You still there. Hello?

(Beat)

VOICE: I am still here.

GLENN: You want something?

VOICE: Mister Cowan, there are rules you need to
follow. Do not take anything back with you that's not
first offered.

GLENN: What does that mean?

VOICE: Do not steal.

GLENN: Ah.

VOICE: No sleeping with your hosts. No goosing. No poking. No grabbing. Don't cop a feel. Remember that the Chinese—most of the people you're going to meet—have never seen an American before. Their reaction—well we don't know what it's going to be. They might just go nuts and surround you. They mean well, but even if they don't, resist fighting. And don't sign anything they give you to sign. Anything. Nothing. Do not sign anything. Do not suddenly decide that this is some kind of platform for you to tell the world how crappy you think it all is. You're an American, Glenn. Understand
If you're approached by someone wanting something or asking questions you must let us know.

GLENN: If like somebody wants to talk to me or something I pick up the phone and just call you. I don't even know you.

VOICE: Speak clearly. We'll be listening.

Scene Eight

(MAO *is showing* NURSE WU *how to play ping pong.* ZHOU *watches.* MAO *is not well, so he struggles.*)

MAO: Hold it like this. You start the topspin low… almost a brush. But that sends the ball high over the net and then it kicks forward, very low. Your opponent expects one kind of bounce and then it's too late.

(MAO *looks at* ZHOU *for reassurance.*)

(MAO *walks away from the table. He is holding some kind of shirt in his hand. In the background* NURSE WU *continues to practice.*)

ZHOU: You do know she was a great player once.

MAO: It's good to discover who will lie to you and who will not.

(ZHOU *has a paper in his hand.* MAO *gives the shirt to* ZHOU *and takes the paper from his hand. He reads. After a moment,* MAO *smiles.)*

MAO: These were his exact words?

ZHOU: Exact words, Chairman. People's Republic of China. First time an American president—

MAO: People's Republic of China.

ZHOU: No more red China. It's clear this was meant for us and not Ceacescu.

MAO: You trust Richard Nixon?

ZHOU: Rightists are easier to deal with. You know just what they think.

MAO: The young man's luggage was checked after he crossed the border?

ZHOU: He had nothing on him.

MAO: But you believe he has a message from the President?

ZHOU: Yes. But he may not know what it is.

(MAO *thinks these things over. Then…)*

MAO: He has a message. It's not in his luggage or person, and he doesn't know what that message is.

ZHOU: Chairman, they were given permission to travel almost immediately. That decision can only come from the President.

(MAO *thinks this over before…)*

MAO: Maybe it's a different message.

(Beat)

(MAO *now reveals the T-shirt. It's the Let it Be T-shirt* GLENN *gave* ZHUANG.)

MAO: This shirt is filthy.

ZHOU: The young man's sweat.

MAO: Foul.

(MAO *hands it to* ZHOU.)

MAO: Examine it again.

(ZHOU *examines it.*)

MAO: Where is it made?

ZHOU: Taiwan.

MAO: What do you make of that?

ZHOU: It's of poor quality.

MAO: It's made by a country that lays claim to ours—
Taiwan. Let it be. The Americans want us to leave
Taiwan alone. (*He starts to go.*)

ZHOU: Whether that's true or not, the Soviets crossed
our border again.

(MAO *stops.*)

ZHOU: We're in talks with Moscow but they continue
to insist Damansky Island—

MAO: Zhenbao Island. It's not theirs.

ZHOU: They insist it's theirs. They've already
positioned troops all around our borders.

MAO: All for a stupid island that is under water half
the year.

ZHOU: They will start there but they won't stop.

MAO: Why would they do this to us.

ZHOU: The Brezhnev Doctrine. They've made it clear
that they can enter any country turning away from
socialism.

MAO: That is what we're doing?

(*Long pause*)

ZHOU: Chairman, to our north and west are the Soviets and they are ready to come in. We have India to the south and Japan to the east. If all our enemies decide to one day come together, what will happen?

(MAO *stops to imagine the possibilities. It's not a pretty picture.*)

ZHOU: Our ancestors taught us to negotiate with faraway countries if we are to protect ourselves from those enemies who now stand at our gates. You said it may have been a mistake to invite the Americans but the Soviets are giving us no other choice.

(*Pause*)

MAO: Continue... (*He starts to go but then stops.*) And get rid of that nasty shirt. I don't ever want to see it again.

(*Blackout*)

Scene Eight-Point-Five

(*On a monitor[s] we see the following:*
DAY THREE
The Great Wall.
"Until you reach the Great Wall, you're no hero." Chairman Mao Tse-tung)

(*Lights shift*)

Scene Nine

(*The South Lawn*)

(*Moonlight. Soon we see* NIXON *in the shadows. He has a basket in hand. Every few moments he bends down. It's not clear what he's doing.*)

(KISSINGER *appears from the darkness. He carries an envelope with him.*)

KISSINGER: May I ask what you're doing, Mister President?

NIXON: I'm hiding the eggs for the egg hunt. I can hide these things better than most.

KISSINGER: For what?

NIXON: It's Easter, Henry. Tomorrow thousands of kids will descend on the South Lawn. Grab a few and follow me.

KISSINGER: Are these real eggs, Mister President?

NIXON: They are, Henry. First time in White House History. Real eggs.

KISSINGER: Mister President, you seem to be making history in all sorts of ways.

NIXON: You're not very funny, Henry.

KISSINGER: An official with the Pakistani embassy was approached by a Chinese diplomat. In the course of the conversation he happened to mention how good you looked during the speech the other night. It's obvious to us he's lying.

NIXON: What do you mean by that?

KISSINGER: We know that it's not your looks he is referring to but your words. The Chinese are responding to your mention of the People's Republic of China. They want to let you know your words were heard.

(NIXON *continues to hide eggs for a few moments.*)

NIXON: You say this with a great deal of confidence, Henry.

KISSINGER: We have a good read on these events.

NIXON: No. No. The other thing. This not being about my looks. How do you know it wasn't my looks he was referring to?

KISSINGER: Mister President, you've already lost an election because of your looks. We know that. It's the honest truth. It falls on us to tell you the truth.

NIXON: Who is we? Who is us?

KISSINGER: Pardon?

NIXON: You say we. We believe. Who's we? It's you. Just you.

KISSINGER: For emphasis.

NIXON: What?

KISSINGER: Emphasis, Mister President. I believe it. But I believe it so strongly that I might as well be a we and not an I.

NIXON: Henry, what did I say about the we. I don't need the emphasis. Stop referring to yourself as we. You're a smart Jew. I know that. But your problem is really the Jewish problem.

KISSINGER: The Jewish problem?

NIXON: You're all insecure. You're all out to prove things. Why say I when you can say we and sound like you got some support. Well you don't, Henry. Oh, now you're upset. Have I upset you? Why are you making that face? Look every people have traits. The Italians? Ever deal with one of them? They don't have their heads screwed on tight. It's a fact that the Irish like to drink. It's also a fact that the Irish get mean after they drink. This is a fact. Now the Jews...Jews can be very aggressive and abrasive and obnoxious. I'm referring to you, Henry. It falls on me to tell you the truth. And I say this as a friend.

(Beat)

KISSINGER: Are you done?

NIXON: For now.

KISSINGER: We believe—I believe this is important for our game with the Soviets. If the Chinese hold the door open for us, then we should do the same.

NIXON: You have a lot to say about this China thing.

KISSINGER: We need it for our game with the Soviets.

NIXON: Yeah, yeah.

KISSINGER: I mean the Soviets would want nothing more than for us to reject this overture.

NIXON: That's the point. That's what they want. For us to slap the Chinese in the face, but we won't, Henry. We will not. Let's not go all Moo Goo Gai Pan here but if they hold the door open for us, than we do the same. *(He hides an egg.)* They'll never find this one. I have places I can hide things and they don't stand a chance of finding them.

(KISSINGER hands NIXON the envelope.)

NIXON: What's in here?

KISSINGER: Pictures are starting to arrive.

NIXON: This ping pong kid has no clue that we're using him?

KISSINGER: After each day is over he surrenders the film. Gladly.

NIXON: Why go so far. Can't our people traveling with them do the same.

KISSINGER: The team may be given more access. Their first meeting with the Premier was a private one. No reporters were allowed.

(NIXON looks at the photographs.)

(Beat)

NIXON: I don't understand how pictures of some chinaman on a bicycle and some ballet thing are going to help us. All this means is that chinamen have no cars and dance like queers.

KISSINGER: There is a third picture.

(NIXON *now sees it.*)

KISSINGER: No American in recent times has come this close to the Premier. He does not look well in it. He may be sick. I am concerned. We believe—

NIXON: Henry.

KISSINGER: I believe the Premier is the one most interested in rapprochement. If something were to happen to him....

NIXON: This could all end.

KISSINGER: It's important we act soon.

NIXON: How do you suggest we do that?

(*Beat*)

(KISSINGER *now hands* NIXON *a piece of paper.*)

KISSINGER: Look over these notes. In a few days you'll be addressing the Society of Newspaper Editors.

NIXON: My favorite people in the world.

KISSINGER: I've made suggestions as to how we can get across to the Chinese that our intentions are real.

(NIXON *looks over the paper. He smiles at* KISSINGER. KISSINGER, *very pleased with himself, smiles back.*)

NIXON: How is the hippie doing?

KISSINGER: He's a good photographer.

NIXON: Henry. (*Beat*) When it's all said done history needs to tell the correct story. My story. A while back I had a talk with Haig and the subject of China came up. I shared with him some of our plans. Your name came up and he mentioned a conversation you had with him a few months into my Presidency. At the time you said—and these were your words—"Al, this cold warrior fellow wants to open relations with China. I think he has lost control of his senses." Did you say that, Henry.

KISSINGER: I would never have said "this cold warrior fellow."

NIXON: That's not what concerns me.

KISSINGER: I did not say any of that.

NIXON: Henry, there are ways I can find out everything said around here. It's possible I read minds. As smart as you think you are, Henry, I know everything about you.

(*An* EASTER BUNNY *enters.*)

KISSINGER: Mister President, there is an easter bunny staring at us.

NIXON: What are you smoking?

KISSINGER: Behind you.

(NIXON *turns.*)

EASTER BUNNY: Don't be alarmed, Mister President, it's me.

NIXON: Petey?

EASTER BUNNY: We're having some of the Secret Service dress as Easter Bunnies tomorrow.

NIXON: That makes sense.

EASTER BUNNY: We think it does, Mister President. I wanted you to see the outfit, so that tomorrow you don't become suspicious when you are followed by Easter bunnies. (*Goes*)

KISSINGER: Look over the statement I've drafted.

(NIXON *studies the paper.*)

(Light shift.)

Scene Ten

(GLENN'*s hotel room.* ZHUANG *is onstage alone. A beat or two.* GLENN *enters from the bathroom.*)

GLENN: I'm just finishing getting ready for the banquet. How do I look?

ZHUANG: You have underwear.

GLENN: Oh yeah. From this part up. This part down I'm still working on. Want to come in?

ZHUANG: Yes.

(GLENN *lets* ZHUANG *in.*)

GLENN: Okay. Welcome. Do you want to speak Chinese or English?

ZHUANG: You speak Chinese?

GLENN: *Ni hao.*

ZHUANG: Let us do English.

GLENN: I'll do my best to keep up.

ZHUANG: Glenn, I need to ask you something.

GLENN: Shoot.

ZHUANG: The sign. What did you do with the sign?

GLENN: The sign?

ZHUANG: Yes.

GLENN: What sign?

ZHUANG: You went walking in streets and you saw a sign. You took sign back here. *(Beat)* It is not yours, Glenn.

GLENN: I thought I'd bring it back as souvenir.

ZHUANG: May you show me.

(GLENN *walks over to the closet and takes out a sign. It has Chinese lettering. As he is doing this...*)

GLENN: I couldn't take back a piece of the Great Wall with me, so I went for this instead. It's not as great as the Wall, which is great but it is—

ZHUANG: Do you know what the signs says, Glenn?

GLENN: It says Glenn Cowan was in China!

ZHUANG: "QUOTATION FROM CHAIRMAN MAO: PEOPLE OF THE WORLD UNITE AND DEFEAT THE U S AGGRESSORS AND ALL THEIR RUNNING DOGS!" *(Beat)* We are trying to be friends.

GLENN: That's right me and you are friends. But friendship is not the same thing as souvenir.

ZHUANG: Our two countries.

GLENN: What about?

ZHUANG: That sign says different.

GLENN: I won't tell anyone where I got it. Just put it up in my bedroom.

ZHUANG: If you travel home with that it will be seen as message response by our government.

GLENN: This is nothing the U S Government hasn't already seen. You go to Berkeley—

ZHUANG: Berk. Lee?

GLENN: The Soviet Union. Only it's in California.

ZHUANG: It's an important place.

GLENN: There's stuff worse than this is all over the campus. If I bring this sign back with me I'll have a line of girls out my door wanting to sleep with Mister Radical.

ZHUANG: You understand, Glenn, that this is bigger than you?

GLENN: No. I don't. Why would you say that?

ZHUANG: Please think about this more.

(The phone rings. After a few rings GLENN *picks up…)*

GLENN: Hello? Hello? *(He hangs up.)* Fine. Fine. It's yours. Take. Our hearts are in the same place.

*(*ZHUANG *takes sign.)*

GLENN: You look great holding that.

ZHUANG: Thank you.

GLENN: You mean it. What that says? You tell me your government and my government are trying to be friends, but what about you. Are you my friend? Or am I just some U S aggressor with some running dogs.

ZHUANG: I do not mean for what this says.

GLENN: Did you ever mean it?

ZHUANG: I don't understand what you ask.

GLENN: It's kind of easy to fall back on that. Not understand. You know what I'm asking.

ZHUANG: I play ping pong. That's all I do.

GLENN: Why did you start?

ZHUANG: I start because I was good.

GLENN: How did you know you were good.

ZHUANG: Because I start and win.

GLENN: Ah, that's the difference. I start because my uncle was throwing an old ping pong table away. No net. I had to imagine it. Not sure what that did other than I had to believe something was there. It's easy now to do that. *(Beat)* Can you help me with the knot. Never done one of these.

ZHUANG: Do you observe how we dress?

GLENN: Grey is in.

ZHUANG: Yes. Grey is in. There are no ties.

GLENN: Okay. Forget the tie. *(He begins to undress and put on his familiar threads. He puts on his yellow hat and studies himself. He tries to find himself in the mirror.)*

(ZHUANG watches him. GLENN notices.)

GLENN: By the way I get that whole thing about keeping people out and building this huge wall but isn't that just the same as keeping people in. You put up a wall and it's you that's not going to get out.

ZHUANG: That is true.

GLENN: I thought so. *(He finishes dressing.)* How do I look now?

ZHUANG: I don't know what to say.

GLENN: That's the look I'm going for. Leave them speechless.

(GLENN goes followed by ZHUANG.)

(Light shift.)

Scene Eleven

(A small Russian restaurant in DC. It's the real thing. If you're not Russian you don't know it exists.)

(KISSINGER is there waiting for something...someone. A RUSSIAN WAITER approaches with a large dish with several appetizers.)

RUSSIAN WAITER: Pickled herrings and onions in sour cream. Pickled beets. Pickled mushrooms. Pickled cabbage. Salo.

KISSINGER: This last one?

RUSSIAN WAITER: It is salo.

KISSINGER: It's not pickled?

RUSSIAN WAITER: It's raw pig fat. Without skin.

(Beat)

KISSINGER: Thank you.

(The RUSSIAN WAITER *now sits down facing* KISSINGER.*)*

(There is a long silence.)

RUSSIAN WAITER: If you visit our country you will see not everything is pickled. We have more to offer. It is important you understand that. Do you understand that?

*(*KISSINGER *now looks around him before turning his attention back to the* RUSSIAN WAITER.*)*

RUSSIAN WAITER: You may choose to go a different way. But that will be a mistake. You will not like what you find there. You will have fried gizzards, shark fin's soup, and fish fillets in pickle wine sauce. You will not like these things. You will regret your decision. You understand what I am saying?

KISSINGER: I have lost my appetite.

RUSSIAN WAITER: They're not willing to negotiate.

KISSINGER: That's a border dispute that does not concern us.

RUSSIAN WAITER: The Chinese can't be trusted.

KISSINGER: Thank you. *(He stands.)*

RUSSIAN WAITER: This young man you have working for you is working hard to make an alliance. I suggest you pull back.

KISSINGER: We have no one working for us. *(He starts to go.)*

RUSSIAN WAITER: Will you like to take the food to go?

(But KISSINGER *is gone.)*

(Lights shift)

Scene Twelve

*(*ZHOU *addresses the Americans.)*

ZHOU: *(In Chinese)* Welcome. We are very happy to have you visit our country.

JIA: *(Translating)* Welcome. We are very happy to have you visit.

ZHOU: *(In Chinese)* This is the beginning of a new chapter in the relations of Chinese and American people.

JIA: *(Translating)* This is the beginning of a new chapter in the relations of Chinese and American people.

ZHOU: *(In Chinese)* I am confident most of our nation supports this new friendship.

JIA: *(Translating)* I am confident most of our nation supports this new friendship.

(Beat)

*(*ZHOU *looks over at* JIA. *She waits for more. Than...)*

(Beat)

ZHOU: *(In broken English)* Welcome Americans.

*(*GLENN *steps forward.)*

GLENN: Mister Premier. Are you familiar with Laurel and Hardy.

*(*ZHOU *hesitates.* JIA *whispers.)*

ZHOU: These are American movie stars.

GLENN: They're always saying, "Well here's another mess you've gotten me into."

ZHOU: This is not mess.

GLENN: No. I know. It's just you and Chairman Mao remind me of those two. They're comedians. They're funny. Ha ha. *(Beat)* Are you going to translate?

(Once again JIA *whispers into* ZHOU's *ear. The one thing we hear is "ha ha".)*

(Beat)

*(*ZHOU *studies* GLENN *for a moment before ignoring this last statement.)*

(Later in the banquet. GLENN *and* ZHOU *find themselves alone.)*

ZHOU: We wish for you to play your very best game

GLENN: What do you think of the hippie movement, Mister Prime Minister?

*(*JIA *whispers the question in Chinese.)*

ZHOU: My answer is not very valuable because I do not have experience of hippie.

GLENN: I'm the first hippie you meet?

ZHOU: Young people will try different things. It's their nature to experiment. When I was your age I lived in France and England. I was learning a little here, a little there. But soon I learned that the minority needs to find something in common with the majority. The majority must be brought over to your side or you will fail. Young man, remember that you are part of a much larger country existing in a much larger world. Careful to not isolate yourself from others, to let the world get away from you. If you do you will find that distance you've created to be an impossible one to return from.

*(*ZHOU *goes leaving* GLENN *to think about this.)*

Scene Thirteen

(On monitor[s]:
"It is not hard for one to do a bit of good. What is hard
is to do good all one's life and never do anything bad, to
act consistently in the interests of the broad masses, the
young people and the revolution, and to engage in arduous
struggle for decades on end. That is the hardest thing of all!"
Chairman Mao Tse-tung)

(GLENN lies in bed reading the Little Red Book. There is a
soft knock on the door. A second knock. He looks around as
he approaches the door. He opens it slowly. JIA is there.)

JIA: Hello, Glenn.

(GLENN looks behind JIA and at the hallway. Nothing. He
ushers her in.)

GLENN: Come in.

JIA: I thought I come and see if you need help.

GLENN: It didn't have to do with—

JIA: This is nice room.

GLENN: The most amazing thing is the toilet. The water
in the toilet goes the opposite direction. Did you know
that? That's what really tells me I'm in China. That's
my proof right there.

JIA: It's not true what you say. China is also in
Northern Hemisphere.

GLENN: Really?

JIA: That does not matter. Water in the same hotel goes
down different drains different directions.

GLENN: It's like we're all the same and it all depends
on the direction we take in life.

JIA: It all depends on the drain.

GLENN: Are you going to tell me what you thought of the note?

JIA: I didn't read.

GLENN: Do you have it with you?

JIA: Yes.

GLENN: Let me see it.

(JIA *gives it to* GLENN. *He opens it and gives it back to her.*)

JIA: You want me to read it now?

GLENN: Go ahead.

(JIA *doesn't. She closes it and gives it back.* GLENN *puts it down.*)

(*She now takes in the room.*)

JIA: Your bags are not packed.

GLENN: I don't pack the night before. In the morning I just toss everything into one bag and I'm ready to roll.

JIA: You forget things that way.

GLENN: What you need you buy when you get there.

JIA: It's not always possible.

GLENN: Look; if you're so worried. Over there is my suitcase. There's stuff all over. Just make sure—

JIA: You're going to very special mountains tomorrow, Glenn.

GLENN: They touch the clouds. Zhuang said an Emperor entered heaven that way. I plan to follow that emperor.

(*During the following* GLENN *walks over to the bar and opens a can of Coca-Cola.*)

GLENN: By the way what's the deal with Taiwan. Enlighten me.

JIA: They've taken land that is ours.

GLENN: Uh-huh. Well whatever happens you guys need to get your hands on Taiwan.

JIA: It will please the Premier to hear you agree with our position.

GLENN: Absolutely. The surfing there is friggin amazing. I have friends who just travel there to go to the beaches on the North Coast. The typhoons head for Japan and you're smoking some heavy river mouth barrels.

JIA: I confess. I understand your friends English but I don't always understand your English.

GLENN: What's that's about?

(By now GLENN has opened a can of Coke and given JIA a drink.)

JIA: Is this the famous Coca-Cola?

GLENN: I have everything I want.

JIA: In hotel for foreign guests.

GLENN: There's some rum in it too. I have a bottle I need to finish if I plan to travel light tomorrow.

JIA: It is very good combination.

GLENN: Lots of people think so.

(The lights go off. Moonlight)

JIA: It is probably loss of power. I will call downstairs. *(She picks up the phone and listens. After a moment or two...)* There is no one there to listen to us.

(GLENN and JIA don't know what to do next. Then...)

GLENN: Before you go I just want to share something with you. *(He finds a joint.)*

JIA: Is that what American cigarettes look like.

GLENN: It's a Mary Jane.

JIA: In America cigarette is Mary Jane?

GLENN: Yeah. Right. Kind of.

JIA: American language is always changing. When I was in school cigarette was cigarette.

GLENN: In America it is custom to share a Mary Jane.

(JIA *hesitates before taking the joint in her hand.*)

GLENN: Nice?

JIA: Yes. It is my very first American cigarette.

GLENN: I'm spoiling you. When do I stop?

(JIA *smiles and smokes more aggressively.*)

GLENN: Hey hey hey. Don't Bogart that joint.

(JIA *doesn't know what* GLENN *means. He just takes the joint out of her hand. During the following they continue to share the joint.*)

JIA: I was very surprised when you put your feet on the ping pong table in order to tie your shoes. I don't think a single person in this country has seen someone do that.

GLENN: I guess that's what this whole cultural exchange thing is about.

JIA: I don't think our countrymen will start to do that.

GLENN: And I don't think we're going to go back and build a Great Wall. That's not the point of cultural exchange. It's all about understanding one another.

JIA: You make a good point.

GLENN: You keep smoking that and you'll see just how smart I become.

JIA: I will.

GLENN: By the way, what did you think? (*Beat*) When I put my foot up on the table and tied my shoes.

JIA: It is very rude. You smile? Why?

GLENN: Because that's not what you thought.

(Beat)

JIA: I thought it must feel good to be able to just do something without consequence. To not feel the world will turn back on you. It is something I do not understand but want to.

GLENN: You want a taste of freedom?

JIA: A taste?

GLENN: It's got a nice taste but an even better aftertaste when nothing happens to you.

(Beat)

JIA: I want more Coca-Cola.

(GLENN *takes* JIA's *glass and walks over to the bar.)*

JIA: With rum. You want to travel light.

(GLENN *starts to make* JIA *a drink.)*

GLENN: Where did you learn English anyway?

JIA: In school.

GLENN: Really?

JIA: Special school where all of us learn different languages. They pick you from when you are four and take you away. You will learn French. And you Russian. You will learn Romanian. I was instructed in English. That upset me because I wanted to learn any language but the language of enemy. The language of people who we would never speak to. For years I thought all my learning would be waste. That all the new words would never go used. I was very lonely inside my head, in your language.

GLENN: I guess what you're trying to say is that I give your life meaning?

JIA: *(Discovering this)* You give my life meaning.

GLENN: I like that. Back home there is nothing like this. *(He grabs the note.)* Do me a favor. Check my grammar.

(JIA hesitates before taking the note. She reads it. Looks at GLENN. Rereads the note.)

JIA: It is correct.

GLENN: Yes! I love it when I get it right.

(JIA moves away to the window.)

JIA: You have view here of everything.

GLENN: Yeah. It's nice.

JIA: If you look across the square—the other side. That is the Zhongnanhai Palace.

GLENN: *(At the window with her)* Over where that long building—

JIA: There is a lake. Yes?

GLENN: I see it.

JIA: And there are a series of residences.

GLENN: They all look the same.

JIA: You see the one with the lights on? The only one with lights in entire city.

GLENN: Yes.

JIA: That is the Chairman's Residence. The lights remain on even in blackout. He reads and reads. It is why he is brilliant and guides us forward.

GLENN: You mean Mao is there right now?

JIA: Yes.

GLENN: Are we going to meet him?

JIA: You may. You may not. The fat one makes decisions at a moment's notice.

GLENN: Did you just say the fat one?

JIA: Did I?

GLENN: You did.

JIA: I did.

(GLENN *and* JIA *laugh for a moment. And then another moment. Before…)*

GLENN: There are no lights on anywhere.

JIA: Most nights power is turned off in the rest of the city.

GLENN: Bummer for you.

JIA: Bummer. Yes. Bummer? What is it this bummer?

GLENN: You ever take acid and it doesn't go well. That's a bum trip.

JIA: What is acid?

GLENN: You mean you've never—

JIA: No.

GLENN: If you think putting your feet up on a table is freedom you need to do acid.

JIA: I think now is my time to go.

GLENN: Alright look. Acid lets you see the thread of things. Nothing makes sense. Not right away. But then you see how everything connects. Something that happens here connects with something happening back home. You understand what I am trying to tell you?

(JIA *shakes her head no.)*

GLENN: Okay. You take acid and you will see how this whole thing is we've been doing—and I mean you, me, Mao, Laurel, Hardy, ping pong, and Everybody—is all one big thing. *(Beat)* Jia, let me make it easy for you.

(GLENN *gently takes the joint from* JIA *and continues to smoke it. He has a piece of perforated paper. He cuts out a small square.)*

GLENN: We don't know how your mind is going to react to being bent but whatever you do, don't fight it.

JIA: This is acid? This will allow me to see the whole picture? What do I do with this paper?

GLENN: Let me have the tip of your tongue. Like this.

(GLENN *sticks his tongue out.* JIA *does the same.*)

GLENN: You look so hot right now.

JIA: What?

GLENN: Stick it back out.

JIA: *(With her tongue out)* What do you want to do—

GLENN: Shhh. No talking with your tongue out.

JIA: What?

GLENN: Stick it out again.

(GLENN *puts one small paper on* JIA*'s tongue.*)

GLENN: Okay. Good. Now stick it back in.

JIA: Now I have taken acid?

GLENN: The trip is just beginning.

JIA: I'm nervous.

GLENN: Let it happen.

(GLENN *takes some. They continue to smoke the joint.*)

JIA: Is it going to happen soon?

GLENN: It will happen when it happens.

JIA: When is that?

GLENN: An hour. Less. Why are you looking at me like that?

JIA: Like what?

GLENN: Like you really want to be completely free of anything and everything.

JIA: It is true that very long ago Chinese men let wives sleep with travellers from foreign lands. At that time foreigners were held in high esteem. Chinese believed foreigners would bring new blood and better future.

GLENN: That's really sweet. Very open minded, you know.

JIA: Do you understand what I say?

GLENN: Are you like telling me that you're like married.

(JIA *nods yes.*)

GLENN: You want me to understand that you're married and you're using me tonight?

JIA: Let me explain—

GLENN: No. No. That's cool. I don't mind being used for tradition and things. I can roll with that.

JIA: It is different than old story. My husband does not know. Even now I am looking for reason to go but can't.

GLENN: You're not in love with him.

(GLENN *kisses* JIA. *Passionately. They get into it but then…*)

JIA: The first lesson one learns when choosing to be translator is that you're always translating two languages not one. There is a literal language but also a second language. The language of action. A kiss is more valuable than someone saying I hate you that same moment. A person waving goodbye is more powerful than same person saying hello. A handshake is more important than any anger that has existed before. Action has its own language and it explains how people who don't understand one another can understand one another. It explains this feeling of knowing you.

(GLENN *kisses* JIA.)

JIA: Why does moon feel so bright on your face?

GLENN: It's a full moon tonight.

JIA: But I can feel the moon when I touch you. It feels like I can touch light and you are source.

GLENN: Groovy.

JIA: Yes. Groovy.

GLENN: Happy trails. I think the acid trip is starting. Another fifteen minutes and we'll be there.

(Somewhere on the stage the following teletype: CONNECTION ESTABLISHED)

(The stage becomes a rainbow of colors before...)

(Blackout)

END OF ACT ONE

ACT TWO

Scene One

(The phone rings. GLENN hesitates before picking it up.)

VOICE: Mister Cowan? Mister Glenn Cowan?

GLENN: This is me.

VOICE: I want you to grab your paddle tennis racket.

GLENN: What?

VOICE: Grab your racket, Mister Cowan.

(GLENN does. Then…)

GLENN: Alright.

VOICE: Mister Cowan, do you know how to hold a pen?

GLENN: Is this a trick question?

VOICE: I want you to use your thumb and index finger to hold the paddle.

(GLENN does.)

VOICE: Are you doing what I'm telling you to do?

GLENN: Yes.

VOICE: Zhuang holds his racket in this fashion. It is called a Chinese penhold grip.

GLENN: I've seen him do it.

VOICE: Our intelligence tells us that the only way to beat him is by forcing him to constantly use his backhand. It will be much harder on his body. Do you understand me so far?

GLENN: You're not telling me anything new.

VOICE: That's when you need to come back inside. You will be playing schizo style.

GLENN: What kind of style.

VOICE: Schizo. It's a new way of thinking that keeps your opponent wondering who is the person standing in front of him. You will find a piece of paper under your door showing you exactly where you need to place that ball.

(A piece of paper is put under the door.)

GLENN: It's this like cheating or something.

(Long pause)

VOICE: It's important you win.

(GLENN picks up the piece of paper. He crumbles it up and tosses it away.)

(Lights shift)

Scene Two

(Lights up)

(Morning light. GLENN sleeps in bed. There are a few lamps scattered about. After a few moments JIA enters from the bathroom. She starts on the mess. Slowly, he is waking up. He notices that she is dressed.)

GLENN: What's wrong? Why are you doing that now?

JIA: I don't want to leave mess behind.

GLENN: There are people who come around and clean up the mess.

JIA: I believe it is us who make mess, us who should clean.

GLENN: You're probably right about that. Now come back to bed.

JIA: I can't.

GLENN: You're going already?

JIA: I must see my mother in the hospital.

GLENN: What's wrong with her?

JIA: It is nothing.

GLENN: She is sick?

JIA: No. She works there. At night. I am there in the morning to walk her home.

GLENN: She can't walk home on her own?

JIA: Why do you assume there is something wrong with her?

GLENN: You're having to meet her—

JIA: Family is important.

GLENN: I know.

JIA: Then my actions should not surprise.

GLENN: They do.

JIA: You don't feel the same?

GLENN: Not always.

JIA: No loyalty to your family?

GLENN: My family thinks I'm a little out of it.

JIA: What is out of it mean?

GLENN: What we did last night. We were out of it for a while. I'm out of it a lot. I'm out of it more than I'm in it.

JIA: You've done a great thing.

GLENN: You mean last night? That's nice of you to say.

JIA: No. This trip.

GLENN: I just got on the wrong bus. Coincidence.

JIA: There is no such thing. You say that clearly last night. All coincidence is connected.

GLENN: Yes. It is. What does that mean? The bus was just waiting around for me. It wasn't an accident.

(Beat)

JIA: It was an accident that was planned.

GLENN: Planned by who?

JIA: Laurel and Hardy.

(The phone rings. And rings. GLENN and JIA freeze a moment. He picks up the phone but there is no one there.)

GLENN: This guy calls me up at night sometimes. He's demanding I win the match with Zhuang. I think it's Henry Kissinger.

JIA: You are getting calls from Henry Kissinger.

GLENN: If we defeat the Chinese—he keeps saying we when it's really me—he thinks afterwards Americans will forget our differences and only remember the win.

JIA: Then you must win.

GLENN: But it's not really about Henry or Mao or America or anything else. It's about me. People back home will forget the person I was and only remember the winner. It's nice, right? That possibility?

(JIA stands and is almost ready to go when…)

JIA: I remember feeling special last night. Does it all go away in the morning?

GLENN: It stays with you.

JIA: Last night was me putting my foot on table and tying my shoes, but now I have to go back to tying my shoes just like everyone else.

GLENN: You don't have to.

JIA: You will too. After big moment always comes little moment. Okay?

GLENN: *(Smiling)* Okay. No. It's not okay. It doesn't have to be that way.

(JIA spots the paddle under the bed.)

JIA: You will need this if you will win.

(JIA gives GLENN the paddle.)

GLENN: I've had this same one since I started. I've lost it but then it finds me. It comes easy for me. Do you think that's been the problem?

JIA: You have problem?

GLENN: I get bored with it. I end up doing other things. This time around I'm not bored. I'm going to beat him but I'm going to have to work for it.

(Children are heard singing a hymn, "Ten Thousand Years to Chairman Mao." The hymn causes JIA to stop for a moment. She listens. She starts to go.)

GLENN: What's wrong?

JIA: It is singing from when I was very little. Time passes but song is the same.

(Lights shift)

Scene Three

(A big banner immediately places us: Annual Convention of the American Society of Newspaper Editors, April 12, 1971 Shoreham Hotel, Washington DC.)

(NIXON *stands in front of a microphone.*)

NIXON: (*Reading from a paper*)
"There was a crooked man and he walked a crooked mile.
He found a crooked sixpence upon a crooked stile.
He bought a crooked cat, which caught a crooked mouse.
And they all lived together in a little crooked house."

(*A* TECHNICIAN *enters.*)

TECHNICIAN: Will that be about as loud as you'll go, Mister President?

NIXON: What the hell does this thing mean you had me read?

TECHNICIAN: Pardon?

NIXON: What is this?

TECHNICIAN: It's a nursery rhyme, Mister President.

NIXON: Why?

TECHNICIAN: We give it to everyone, so as to get a good sense of tone, voice strength. Is that as loud as you'll go?

NIXON: Yes.

TECHNICIAN: Great. Thank you.

(*Quick light shift*)

(*Lights come up high on* NIXON *at the podium. A loud murmur. Then…*)

(NIXON addresses a group of reporters.

NIXON: I wish the ping pong team well. I understand they're playing some exhibition matches. I wish both teams well. Clearly, this trip is significant. More significant for you people than anyone else.
My understanding—and I haven't had time to really study the transcript—is that the Premier extended

American journalists an invitation to visit the People's
Republic of China, so if nothing else comes of this
it seems to me this invitation will allow the regular
American access to a country that's remain closed for
over twenty years. Yesterday my two daughters were
at the White House to help us celebrate Easter. Tricia
was there with Eddie—they're getting married this
summer. The talk turned to the honeymoon. Where
should we go, they wanted to know. They wondered
where Pat and I would go if we were to have a second
honeymoon. I thought about this for a while and
finally—this was after some time—I said the place to
go is Asia. I hope that sometime in your life sooner
rather than later you will be able to go to China to see
the great cities and the people. I hope they do. As a
matter of fact, I hope sometime I do.

(Cameras off. Lights off)

(Blackout)

Scene Four

(The zoo in Beijing. GLENN *and* ZHUANG. *They are looking
at a panda.)*

ZHUANG: He is the oldest panda. It is born in 1949.
Same year of our country.

GLENN: You're putting me on.

ZHUANG: What?

GLENN: That panda bear is as old as China.

ZHUANG: People's Republic of China.

GLENN: Yeah. Yeah. That one there is…well that makes
this place twenty-one. This place is twenty-one years
old?! Wow. You're nine years away from thirty!

ZHUANG: Is that bad?

GLENN: That's good! That's good. You don't want to be thirty.

ZHUANG: I am almost thirty.

GLENN: Thirty is when you have to choose who you're going to be the rest of your life. If you don't do it by thirty then They choose for you.

ZHUANG: Who is they?

GLENN: They is like The System.

ZHUANG: We have chosen. We are communists.

GLENN: There you go. And you're only twenty-one. That's impressive. We're almost three hundred years old and we can't get our shit together.
I want to ask you something. Listen to me. Just. That meeting on the bus. When we first met. That was real, right?

ZHUANG: Yes. It happened.

GLENN: I know it happened! I was there.

ZHUANG: What are you asking?

GLENN: The drugs do their own thing and take you to these special places, but our encounter involved no drugs. It was a peak experience without drugs.

ZHUANG: It was real.

GLENN: Of course it was real. What am I asking you for? It happened. Yes. Good. Of course. *(Beat)* It changed my life, Zhuang.

ZHUANG: I am a little lost.

GLENN: I have my family back. I talked to my mother. I hadn't talked to her in what six months, a year? Now she's on the phone with me. I have her back. I could tell she was smiling on the other end. Her crazy son is doing something with his life. I've become a politician or something. I'm what I want to be and I'm not thirty.

I beat The System! That meeting on the bus was the start of it. It happened because things aligned and now a string holds us together. It's going to hold us together forever. You may go your own way but that string is going to pull you right back to me. We're the same story. A real story about strangers coming together and becoming friends. *(Beat)* You are my friend.

ZHUANG: Glenn, tomorrow we play match in front of many people.

GLENN: I haven't stopped thinking about it.

ZHUANG: It is important day for our two countries. Americans will watch. Glenn, I was told by your players that maybe you are not well.

GLENN: Who said that?

ZHUANG: It does not matter. I was asked to talk to you.

GLENN: I've been clean for four hours now.

ZHUANG: Clean?

GLENN: No drugs. Nothing.

ZHUANG: You have drugs with you. People are looking.

GLENN: It's a zoo. What do you expect people to do.

ZHUANG: Mellow out, Glenn.

GLENN: Did you just say—what did you just say?

ZHUANG: Mellow out.

GLENN: I taught you that.

ZHUANG: Yes.

GLENN: I'm fucking proud of myself.

ZHUANG: They're looking, Glenn.

GLENN: That's because we're famous.

ZHUANG: It is because of your dress.

GLENN: What?

ZHUANG: They look because your outfit.

GLENN: They look because the world hasn't seen the likes of us. *(Shouting out to the crowd)* Give peace a chance! *(Back to* ZHUANG*)* That's exactly what we did.

ZHUANG: Do you need help, Glenn?

GLENN: If I need help ever I'm coming to you. I expect you to do the same. Look! Another one.

ZHUANG: Taotao. He is youngest.

GLENN: Look at him grab. Reminds me of my niece when she was one. She'd grab on to anything she could get her hands on. She'd grab on hard and not let go.

*(*GLENN *and* ZHUANG *look at the second panda. Then…)*

*(*GLENN *gets no response. He turns to watch the panda.* ZHUANG *studies him. Then…)*

ZHUANG: You have brought color with you, Glenn.

GLENN: What's that?

ZHUANG: Color. I don't remember ever seeing color on someone. Until you. *(Beat. In Chinese)* Thank you.

(Blackout)

Scene Five

(Night. Total darkness. Very faint light coming from a night lamp. ZHOU *and* MAO *are there but we can barely make them out. Two familiar voices:)*

ZHOU: Chairman, where is your nurse?

MAO: In the wastebasket of our nation.

ZHOU: This is your third in as many months.

MAO: What is the news?!

ZHOU: We've been made aware of a speech President Nixon made last week. In it he mentions his daughter's coming honeymoon. He advised his daughter that the place to go is China. He then went further saying he wished to come to China.

MAO: Did the American press pick up on it?

ZHOU: No. The recent attacks on Ban Dong have kept the American press busy. I believe the President knew this would be the case, and so he used the opportunity to talk to us directly without others listening.

(MAO *starts to cough.*)

ZHOU: Your lungs are working. That is a good sign.

MAO: I'm coughing blood.

ZHOU: Its best I come another time. You need to sleep.

MAO: I don't have much time left.

(MAO *pulls off one or two needles.* ZHOU *stops him.*)

ZHOU: If you refuse your treatments—

MAO: I will live another five minutes. What is five minutes when I need another lifetime.

ZHOU: The drugs work.

MAO: They make me see things that are not there.

ZHOU: They give you life.

MAO: They give me a different life.

ZHOU: You will be fine.

MAO: What is wrong with me?

ZHOU: Your pulse is very weak, Chairman. You have a lung infection. Your heart needs full attention.

MAO: Is that all?

ZHOU: You have too much fluid in your body, your neck and forehead are swollen.

MAO: But is that all?

ZHOU: Without the drugs nothing can be done.

(MAO stops. He lets the drugs continue to work.)

(There is a subtle change in the Chairman. Is he getting better? Is it a smile? Bliss? A few moments of this before…)

MAO: I will like to invite the President of the United States to come for a visit.

ZHOU: Chairman.

MAO: The Soviets are more annoying.

ZHOU: You must rest before making this decision.

MAO: This boy is very likable. He will bring good will back home with him. His President is ready.
He wants a second honeymoon—a second chance.
Let's give him one. Purpose is the only drug I need.

Scene Six

(The West Sitting Room)

(The only thing unusual is a large T V with its guts spilled out onto the floor. KISSINGER studies the broken T V—he's on his knees.)

(NIXON has been drinking. He's done this throughout the play but it is most noticeable in this scene.)

KISSINGER: It's broken.

NIXON: I didn't know that, Henry. I'm so glad I have you to state the obvious.

(After a moment, a WHITE HOUSE AIDE leads a young man in. He's Chinese-American.)

WHITE HOUSE AIDE: He's arrived, Mister President.

NIXON: *(Without looking back at the aide)* Good. That's all.

(The WHITE HOUSE AIDE goes.)

(NIXON *is still not looking over at the technician*)

KISSINGER: Mister President.

NIXON: How are they so good at this? Nothing more to do there than just pick up a damn paddle and start playing.

KISSINGER: Mister President.

(KISSINGER *points over at the* TECHNICIAN.)

NIXON: You're Chinese.

TECHNICIAN: My parents came over from China.

NIXON: You're Chinese.

KISSINGER: He's Chinese.

TECHNICIAN: I'm Chinese.

(Beat)

NIXON: You play ping pong?

TECHNICIAN: No.

NIXON: Don't all Chinamen play it?

TECHNICIAN: No.

NIXON: What are you standing there for. Fix the damn T V.

(The TECHNICIAN *starts working on the T V.* KISSINGER *hovers over him.)*

KISSINGER: Shouldn't that red wire—

(The TECHNICIAN *gives* KISSINGER *a look.)*

KISSINGER: I'm telling you. That red wire maybe needs to—

NIXON: Let him do his job, Henry.

TECHNICIAN: What is this? Some kind of tape recorder?

NIXON: Give me that!

TECHNICIAN: What's it doing in here?

NIXON: What are you accusing me of?

(Beat)

TECHNICIAN: Mister President, can you tell me exactly what happened—

NIXON: I'm watching the 49ers/ Redskins and the next moment. Done. Broken.

TECHNICIAN: This broke down in December?

NIXON: Yes.

TECHNICIAN: It's April, Mister President.

NIXON: No fucking kidding. Is it really?

TECHNICIAN: You haven't had it fixed since?

NIXON: Why don't you just say what's on your mind! Get it over with! If you're going to accuse me of something do it now.

KISSINGER: He just wants to know if you've had it fixed once already.

NIXON: Why would I do that? Football season ended that day. 49ers sent the Skins packing.

TECHNICIAN: I saw that game. Heartbreaker.

NIXON: You watch football?

TECHNICIAN: Yes.

NIXON: American football? Not the kind they kick a ball around until someone does something with it.

TECHNICIAN: I was born here.

NIXON: Then you saw the Skins blow it. They were on the eight yard line and wanted to put the game away.

TECHNICIAN: That's not the kind of football they play.

NIXON: That's why they called it! It was the right call.

TECHNICIAN: They lost thirteen yards on the play. It was the wrong call.

NIXON: Nobody expected them to make that call.

TECHNICIAN: The Niners did.

NIXON: You look brilliant if it goes your way, an ass if it doesn't. It should have worked.

TECHNICIAN: Did you see the way they played after that—

NIXON: The T V broke.

TECHNICIAN: Wait. After that play was when the T V broke?

NIXON: What do you do when you're not fixing T Vs? You watch football. That much we know. But your parents or friends. What do they do for fun?

KISSINGER: They do tai chi and play mahjong.

NIXON: Shut up.

TECHNICIAN: We watch T V.

NIXON: Is that right? You hear what this man does? This is diplomacy here, Henry. This is where we learn what they're really like. What else do you do? What do Chinese people like to do? Let me ask you this. If one day say someone were to visit China—

KISSINGER: I don't think we should discuss this.

NIXON: —what would be an appropriate gift?

TECHNICIAN: Mister President, I have no one in China. My family left before the communists.

NIXON: Lucky for them. Lucky for you. But now what would you say if you were to visit. What would you do?

(*The* TECHNICIAN *now rises.*)

NIXON: A handshake. That's appropriate, correct?

TECHNICIAN: Yes.

(NIXON *extends his hand but* KISSINGER *intervenes.*)

NIXON: Then what? A handshake. What's next?

TECHNICIAN: I've never been to China.

NIXON: This is your chance. You wait and you won't be able to. You won't have a chance to enjoy it. It's now. It can't wait any longer.

TECHNICIAN: It's not possible for me to ever go.

NIXON: That's not good. That attitude. If you were to go—

KISSINGER: Have you used your high voltage probe to check if you have anything.

TECHNICIAN: First thing I tried.

KISSINGER: Horizontal output tube?

TECHNICIAN: It has some drive. The tube is not hot to the touch. I've tried everything.

KISSINGER: Can I see the schematic?

TECHNICIAN: You think I haven't tried everything.

KISSINGER: You've been here five minutes and you've tried everything? Let me have the schematic.

(NIXON *looks the* TECHNICIAN *over. And over. He circles him.*)

NIXON: Are you a 49ers fan?

TECHNICIAN: What?

NIXON: You're a 49ers fan! (*Beat*) You're a 49ers fan and you're a liar.

TECHNICIAN: I'm a Redskins fan.

NIXON: I recognize a liar when I see one. Get the fuck out.

(TECHNICIAN *starts to go.*)

KISSINGER: Leave the screwdriver.

(TECHNICIAN *does and goes.*)

NIXON: These chinks. They have a temper. Don't let them fool you.

(KISSINGER *begins to work on the T V.*)

NIXON: What is that button for?

KISSINGER: It's not a button. It's a base that directs power back over here. Without it all power would remain to the one side and never travel beyond. There needs to be balance.

NIXON: Have you fixed many T Vs?

KISSINGER: It's logic.

NIXON: So now what are you doing?

KISSINGER: I'm screwing a screw.

NIXON: A regular screw?

KISSINGER: There is no such thing. All screws are special. *(Beat)* I think it will work now.

NIXON: You're just going to leave all those wires hanging out like that?

KISSINGER: I didn't say the back was going to look pretty, but there will be a picture. *(He turns it to us.)*

NIXON: And it's going to work even with that crack?

KISSINGER: Yes.

NIXON: Let's see. Turn the damn thing on.

(KISSINGER *plugs the T V in and turns it on. It works.*)

(*Quick light change.* KISSINGER *and* NIXON *remain on in a faint light but now we see the last few moments of the ping pong match. It's fast...almost violent.*)

(*A cheer.* GLENN *wins.*)

(*Moments later the lights have shifted back to* KISSINGER *and* NIXON.)

(*Silence*)

(The T V breaks down. Sparks and explosions)

(Long pause)

KISSINGER: Well this has worked on an R C A before. It is obvious to me Zenith does things differently.

NIXON: Yes. Obvious now. It would have been nice to have known that before. *(He walks away. Beat)* How many people are in there watching, ten, fifteen thousand maybe?

KISSINGER: Likely a higher number.

NIXON: And they all cheered when he won. That wouldn't have happened even two years ago. But it's two years later and everything we've worked for is right there in one cheer. Next is up to us. *(He looks straight into KISSINGER's eyes.)* Do you know football, Henry?

KISSINGER: Of course.

NIXON: Stupid question of me because you know everything; but have you ever been to a game? Not just T V but actually been there…with the fans. The noise, you know. The excitement.

KISSINGER: It is a thrill I have not experienced.

NIXON: These idiots who call the game too violent, they don't know it's just a chess game. It's all strategy. You have a game plan. You think about things ahead of time, but if you're not flexible, too set in your ways, you're going to lose.

KISSINGER: Football makes sense.

NIXON: I want to win this one, but we're making it up as we go along, aren't we? What do you think the Russians will do when we accept Mao's invitation?

KISSINGER: He has not invited us.

NIXON: That cheer you heard. That's our invitation. It's coming. The rest is up to us.

KISSINGER: I believe the Russians will increase their presence in North Vietnam.

NIXON: I don't want to be pulled into it further.

KISSINGER: You do not have to, but you will lose Vietnam.

NIXON: I say yes to the Chinese now and I lose Vietnam?

KISSINGER: It may just come down to that.

NIXON: Not necessarily. If we get the Chinese over to our side—

KISSINGER: That is a possibility but not likely.

NIXON: There is still one option.

(Beat)

KISSINGER: The world doesn't have enough level headed people leading it for that to be an option.

NIXON: A nuclear bomb on the North Vietnamese would certainly make me even less popular with the press.

KISSINGER: I would imagine.

(Beat)

NIXON: What's in it for us? What do we really gain by accepting Mao's invitation?

KISSINGER: In the end peace with China will spare millions.

(NIXON *thinks this over.*)

KISSINGER: And the Soviets will piss their pants.

(Beat)

NIXON: I made that call, Henry.

KISSINGER: What call?

NIXON: The playoffs. George Allen is a good friend of mine—the coach. I called him during the game. He took the call. I told him they weren't expecting the reverse. It's a play I saw him run in practice. I made that call, Henry. They read the play almost immediately. They anticipated it. How? I don't know. Allen called the play and it cost them the game. I took a chance and we lost everything.

KISSINGER: This is not football, Mister President.

NIXON: No fucking kidding, Henry.

KISSINGER: If you don't take this chance you may not have another. Eventually the Soviets and the Chinese will work out their differences. We have to get their first.

NIXON: Or we're fucked. *(Beat)* Wait three days. On April 14th we'll officially announce the lifting of trade restrictions. That's our yes to the invitation that will come soon after.

KISSINGER: It is as their Premier says.

NIXON: What's that?

KISSINGER: The little ball moves the big ball. *(He starts to exit.)*

NIXON: Henry.

KISSINGER: What is it?

(Pause)

NIXON: You know there was a time Eisenhower wouldn't meet with me when I was his Vice President. That's how I ended up learning to play golf. Only way I'd get to him. He used me, you know. He used me to get elected. I was the mudslinger and he was the all squeaky-clean general. Just imagine that. People more afraid of a Quaker than a five star general. But that's

always been the case with me. I've been the one people
don't like. I've been the asshole. *(Beat)* Don't ever try
taking on a new self, Henry. Not for a five star general
or some other asshole because it sticks. That's it. Your
new self. That's who you will always be. Unless. When
something this big comes along what people think
of you changes. It's possible. You go from asshole to
statesman. It's possible to change the way people look
at you, isn't it.

(Slow shift out)

Scene Seven

*(A locker room. Offstage we hear a contest of some kind
going on. The roar of the crowd punctuates the entire scene.)*

(On stage are ZHUANG *and* GLENN. GLENN *is on his feet
and pacing;* ZHUANG *is calm. Their shirts are soaked in
sweat.)*

*(The only other interesting thing is a life-size portrait of
 MAO with ping pong paddle. You could say that the scene
has a third character.)*

GLENN: Why did you do it?

ZHUANG: I don't know what you want.

*(*GLENN *is angry. During the following he smashes a locker
with the racquet and kicks a chair over.)*

GLENN: What do you mean it wasn't you. You threw
the match. You pretended to lose.

ZHUANG: That is not true.

GLENN: You fucking let me win. That's just not cool.

ZHUANG: It was real game.

GLENN: I expected the best of you.

ZHUANG: I did give you best.

GLENN: You gave me shit! You gave me lies! You made it so that you stayed close but you let me win. *(He walks over to the ping pong table.)* Come on now. Let's play for real.

ZHUANG: That was real game.

GLENN: Okay. One more time then. Rematch. Your chance to beat me. Come on. Stand up. What are you doing? Stand.

ZHUANG: We are finished.

GLENN: I want the best of you.

ZHUANG: You had me.

GLENN: Why are you lying to me? No one is here. Come on. Let's play. Say fuck you to the fat man looking at us right now, fuck you to the little skinny guy and fuck you to everyone else and bring it on. Right here. This is it. This is our space. No one else but us.

(GLENN tosses ZHUANG a racket, but he tosses it back.)

GLENN: What do you have to lose?

ZHUANG: Everything.

(GLENN begins calming down.)

GLENN: You don't want to because you're afraid of the truth. You're afraid I'll really beat you. You're afraid of me.

ZHUANG: I am not.

(A big roar)

GLENN: *(Calmly, he tries a different way to get to ZHUANG)* This one was decided before we even started playing.

ZHUANG: There is always loser for winner to exist, Glenn. Those rules never seem to change. *(He walks over to his locker.)*

GLENN: Just say yes. That's all. Say it. I'm just trying
to tell you how good you are. I mean I'm good but…
maybe one out of ten times I can do it.

ZHUANG: Today was one out of ten.

GLENN: Fuck you. Asshole. When you're ready for the
truth then find me. The fucking string I talked to you
about, no more.

(GLENN *walks over to his locker and begins to change.
Meanwhile we see* ZHUANG *struggle with his locker. He's
locked out. Suddenly,* ZHUANG *hits the locker hard. At this
moment* GLENN *stops what he is doing.*)

GLENN: What is it?

ZHUANG: Locked.

GLENN: You don't have the key.

ZHUANG: I don't know where it is.

GLENN: You lost it?

(ZHUANG *nods yes.*)

GLENN: It's not a big deal, bro. Watch and learn. (*He
works on the lock. Pop. He opens it.*) It's that easy.

ZHUANG: It is not.

(GLENN *walks over and begins changing.* ZHUANG *stares at
his locker, the lock. He begins softly…*)

ZHUANG: Many years ago Mao pick up a pin-pong
paddle. He tell Chinese people "Regard ping pong
ball as head of the capitalist enemy. Hit it with
your socialist bat and you have won the point for
fatherland." Mao make table tennis national obsession.
I was star. I won world championships in '61, '63, and
'65.

(*By now* GLENN *is listening*)

ZHUANG: Then one day Mao get old, put down
his ping-pong paddle, and told everyone to do the

same. He sent national team to countryside to learn something of real value to Revolution. The Cultural Revolution. I end up in prison. *(He hesitates.)* I was alone for three years in cell with no one. My family believes I am no more. My guards believe I can't read English so to torture they throw book in English in cell. I read Count of Monte Cristo. "All human wisdom is contained in these two words—Wait and Hope."

GLENN: How did you get out?

ZHUANG: One ordinary day that was no different than every other day before that one they open door. I look around for damage. Three of my teammates had committed suicide. Six months later we travel to Japan.

GLENN: Six months ago you were in jail?

ZHUANG: Wait and hope. Wait and wait for something, a person. I wait for you, Glenn, and I did not know. I hoped for you.

GLENN: What have I done?

ZHUANG: You helped them find some use for me again.

(GLENN is flattered and pleased. He hugs ZHUANG but he resists.)

GLENN: Something wrong?

ZHUANG: Listen to full story, Glenn.

(GLENN steps back.)

ZHUANG: I want to say now you are my friend. You say before. What you say? A string.

GLENN: Exactly.

ZHUANG: Listen. Forgive. I was given a special gift to carry with me to Japan. I was told to give it to American player who will most value it.

GLENN: I don't understand what you're saying.

ZHUANG: Premier took me aside and told me I must make friend with American.

GLENN: The whole thing? The bus—

ZHUANG: Our bus waited patient for you to leave practice. We know you will run for any bus.

GLENN: You guys were just sitting around waiting for some sucker like me to walk in.

ZHUANG: I didn't know purpose of plan but it was planned.

GLENN: This was all a set up. Nothing genuine about this?

ZHUANG: Yes. Real. I was told to become friend but now I am your friend.

GLENN: You were told to.

ZHUANG: Yes but different now.

GLENN: You were told to just like you were told to let me win. You do what you're told.

ZHUANG: I do what I'm told because my life will always depend on it.

(Beat)

GLENN: I'm leaving tomorrow. I have so many memories but this is what I'm leaving with?

ZHUANG: You are innocent. You know nothing but innocent game that for you is always innocent game. A game that is good to you. Always. But it is game. Fun. It is no more than politics for me. The reason I start playing a long time ago is lost for me.

(Lights shift)

Scene Eight

(A dim light remains on GLENN *and* ZHUANG.*)*

*(*NIXON *addressing Americans from the White House.)*

NIXON: "I have requested this television time tonight to announce a major development in our efforts to build a lasting peace in the world.

As I have pointed out on a number of occasions over the past three years, there can be no stable and enduring peace without the participation of the People's Republic of China and its 750 million people. That is why I have undertaken initiatives in several areas to open the door for more normal relations between our two countries.

The announcement I shall now read is being issued simultaneously in Peking and in the United States:"

(Lights shift)

Scene Nine

(Air Force One. NIXON *sits alone and looking out the cabin window. He practices using a pair of chopsticks. It's almost childlike. Near him is Pat Nixon's famous red coat.)*

(Silence. Just the roar of the plane. Time passes.)

(The PILOT *enters.)*

PILOT: Mister President, we've just received the all clear. We'll have you down on the ground in about six minutes.

NIXON: Thank you.

*(*PILOT *exits.)*

*(*KISSINGER *enters. He has a notebook with him. For a moment* NIXON *stops trying to work the chopsticks.)*

NIXON: The first time I met Pat I told her I was going to marry her. I've always gotten what I wanted.

(KISSINGER *lets the moment rest before…*)

KISSINGER: Mister President.

NIXON: How have I managed to do it all? You're smart. Explain it to me. Explain to me how I've been able to get everything I've ever wanted. *(Pause. He looks out the window. He seems distracted.)*

KISSINGER: Mister President.

NIXON: What is it, Henry?

KISSINGER: I've listed Taiwan as the second most important point.

NIXON: Good. *(He picks up the chopsticks again. He is still having trouble with them.)*

KISSINGER: Just take that second one and put it between the tip of your thumb and index finger. It's the correct way.

NIXON: Henry.

KISSINGER: Yes, Mister President?

(NIXON *is about to tell* KISSINGER *to fuck off but then changes his mind. The pull of the window is too great.)*

KISSINGER: I also wanted to let you know. The Soviets have just invited you to Moscow. As you clearly stated, they're pissing their pants.

(Beat)

NIXON: What's this I hear about Dinah Shore.

KISSINGER: We're just friends, Mister President.

NIXON: Not you! My daughter told me the kid was on her show.

KISSINGER: I will ask Dinah next time we have dinner.

NIXON: The kid was going on about our trip. He wants to take credit for it.

KISSINGER: A year ago there was no hope.

NIXON: It's an I, Henry.

KISSINGER: What would you like to do?

NIXON: I'd like him to go away.

KISSINGER: Go where, Mister President?

(NIXON waves him off but KISSINGER stays put. The next few moments are a quieter NIXON. He may be different but he's still the same.)

NIXON: Henry, The New York Times is going to come to you for a quote. You don't say a fucking word to them. The blackout against the Times remains in effect.

KISSINGER: I will not talk to *The New York Times.*

NIXON: They're all Jews if you notice—I don't want you talking to any of them. They want to take me down but...

(NIXON notices KISSINGER really listening and decides to stop himself. NIXON waves KISSINGER off.)

KISSINGER: Mister President, you mentioned something about being Eisenhower's mudslinger. No one made you do that. You wanted this, so you did that. *(Beat)* Congratulations.

(KISSINGER exits leaving the President alone. NIXON continues to look out the window.)

(Lights shift)

Scene Ten

(GLENN *is standing on the tarmac.* JIA *enters.*)

GLENN: There are no planes.

JIA: What?

GLENN: We're in an airport. Where are the airplanes?

JIA: It is important that this is only flight this day.

GLENN: No kidding. They can just stop traffic.

JIA: Why does that surprise you?

GLENN: I guess I'm really important.

JIA: They wait inside for last picture.

GLENN: I wasn't sure if I'd see you again.

JIA: Wherever the Premier goes I follow. I made that clear.

GLENN: Ah. Yeah. Okay. So that explains who that third person was in bed with us.

JIA: That night I didn't follow.

GLENN: Oh no?

JIA: You're upset.

GLENN: What did you want from me? What were you looking to find out?

JIA: I was curious.

GLENN: Yeah. No I get that. Curious about what? About me? About what I know.

JIA: It was you who sent note to me. Do you remember?

GLENN: Did you share it with other people. Chinese wives sleep with other men to what...get at their hearts, so that they can discover some truths about them. Something useful to use for what?

JIA: Do you listen to what you say?

GLENN: I walked out of school and never went back because I knew I had to go find something for myself. Something real. Something that had meaning that went beyond any drug. Okay. Tell me this. At least tell me what this is about. You planned it all but for what?

JIA: I must go inside.

GLENN: Why? He can handle himself. He speaks English.

JIA: I was told to come get you for final picture. It is too cold out here.

GLENN: They showed that match on T V back at home. People saw me win. People think I'm something now. But I'm not going back any different than I came. So where does that leave me? I only have two choices, Jia. Go back and live the lie or stay here and continued to be lied to.

JIA: Return to your family.

GLENN: They'll be the first to figure it out because it won't take long before the real me pops back out. *(He takes a breath before…)* I turned thirty on this trip. I told no one. I thought if I make it out of here a different person then it doesn't matter. *(Beat)* There ain't no other China in my future, Jia. This is it. This WAS it

JIA: You are different because I am different.

GLENN: What's that mean?

JIA: I changed that night. I say for you to accept that night as true.

GLENN: Alright. Then I stay. I can get anything I want here. In China. It's easy enough. I stay with you.

JIA: That is not possible, Glenn.

GLENN: Okay. Come back with me. Leave right now. On that plane. I'll sneak you in. You told me you don't always understand what I'm saying. You're not the only one, Jia. You come with me, learn my language, and whenever I need someone to help them understand me—and I know I'm going to need help— there you are.

JIA: It is too late for me to learn another language.

GLENN: Do you know what daytime television is.

JIA: Yes. Television in the day.

GLENN: That's right. I've been promised a show. I'm going to be all over the T V. Someone called about wanting me to write a book. Another guy keeps insisting I need a manager. I'm going to be a big star. I'm going to be a big liar and a big star. Where are you going?

JIA: I will wait inside for you to come to take last picture.

GLENN: Fuck you. You want my picture than pay for it. Or tell me what this is about. Oh, before I forget. *(He takes out the silk weaving and opens it.)* I've had enough of China.

(GLENN gives JIA the silk weaving.)

JIA: What are you doing?

GLENN: It's yours. Take it. Or give it to Zhuang. Or trash it.

JIA: It was a gift.

GLENN: It can't be a gift if it was a lie.

(JIA realizes the truth in GLENN's statement and exits with the weaving.)

(Slowly Just My Imagination fades in and fades out.)

Scene Eleven

(A diner. Mostly empty. AUBREY, *in her waitress uniform, wanders over and watches the T V. On it* NIXON *is resigning the Presidency.)*

*(*GLENN *enters almost unrecognizable. His hair is longer, messier. The facial hair and oversize clothes hide a dissipated body. He drags a large suitcase.)*

*(*AUBREY *turns to him when he's almost on top of her. She is startled but quickly recognizes* GLENN.*)*

GLENN: Hey.

AUBREY: Glenn.

*(*GLENN *nods yes.)*

(The COOK *looks back but soon is paying attention to* NIXON. *For a while we hear the President. The two are drawn to the announcement. Then...)*

GLENN: Are you ready?

AUBREY: What for?

GLENN: It's time. We're leaving.

AUBREY: Glenn, does anyone know you're here.

GLENN: Everyone.

AUBREY: Your mother called me last week saying you've been showing up at teammates' houses.

GLENN: Whatever she said to you—

AUBREY: You're not well, Glenn. How did you get out of the hospital?

GLENN: I wasn't in a hospital. Now let's go.

AUBREY: There is no going anywhere.

GLENN: China. This is it. Life magazine paid for an exclusive. This is a once in a lifetime chance. What are you doing just standing around for? We have to go now.

AUBREY: That was a long time ago.

GLENN: It's now. Come on.

AUBREY: We play ping-pong, Glenn. And for some reason we happen to have gotten lucky and be at the center of some world event, but that all came to an end a long time ago. *(Beat)* Is there someone I can call?

GLENN: What's he saying?

AUBREY: He's resigning.

GLENN: Why?

AUBREY: You don't know?

GLENN: I've been busy, you know. Interviews. Talk shows. Carson. He smokes between commercials. He smokes and doesn't look at you. Is it that hard for you to look at me? *(Beat)* All that stuff eats away at my time. I don't know how I even came here but—

AUBREY: Glenn, it's been years. That's the past.

(Beat)

GLENN: It's over?

AUBREY: What?

(GLENN points over to the T V.)

AUBREY: It's over, yes.

GLENN: It was me, you know. I got him there. He never called me. He never said thank you. He never did. *(A while and then…)* If I had seen those mountains for myself I would have touched heaven.

(A faint light on ZHUANG)

ZHUANG: We tried to wake you but you were passed out drunk. I wanted you to see them for yourself. We all did. We tried everything but you were gone.

GLENN: I would have changed forever. I wouldn't be me. I wouldn't be this. I had a chance. *(Pointing at the T V)* I wouldn't be him.

AUBREY: Glenn. I was there. I saw those mountains for myself. I stood there and waited...waited for you. And then when I saw you were not coming I just waited. *(Beat)* It didn't do anything for me, Glenn. I'm still here. I'll be here. You can always find me.

GLENN: You were afraid they wouldn't let you out. They opened the door and left it wide open.

(GLENN takes a few steps and then the suitcase pops open. Inside are books...lots of books. They're the same book. On the cover a young and handsome Glenn is swinging a racquet. AUBREY helps him pick up the books.)

GLENN: What do you think of the picture?

AUBREY: You look good.

GLENN: It's me. *(He holds it next to his face.)* It's me. It's on sale now. You go to any bookstore—

AUBREY: It's been a while since—those are just remainders.

GLENN: You have a pen. Let me have that.

(AUBREY gives GLENN the pen. He writes something in it and autographs it. He looks back up at the T V one last time. NIXON rambles on.)

GLENN: It's over. *(Beat)* You take care of yourself. I'll be seeing you soon.

(AUBREY disappears.)

(NIXON appears. GLENN and NIXON now stand in separate lights.)

(Faintly we can see ZHOU and a few Chinese delegates.)

ZHOU: "Your handshake comes over the vastest ocean in the world—twenty-five years of no communication."

(ZHOU *and delegates disappear.*)

GLENN: Mister President?!

NIXON: Mister Cowan.

GLENN: Yes. Me. That's right. Me.

NIXON: If it weren't for you…a great American.

(NIXON *puts his hands on* GLENN*'s shoulders.*)

GLENN: If only you were real.

NIXON: I am.

GLENN: If only I were real.

NIXON: You are.

GLENN: If only this whole thing had really happened.

NIXON: *(Sadly)* It did. For both of us.

(*Lights fade slowly to…*)

END OF PLAY